5 . . .

4 . . .

3 . . .

2 . . .

1 . . .

WRITE!

25 Speculative Fiction Writing Prompts

By Tyrean Martinson

Contents

INTRODUCTION

As a writer, I have blank page days, where I struggle to start with the "right" words or the "right" idea. Many writers call this "Writer's Block" and some even find it impossible to conquer. I think it's always possible to conquer. Sometimes, we just have to have confidence in our own words and ideas. At other times, we need to use writing prompts to get us started. Writing prompts can be as complex as whole scenarios with characters and dilemmas, or they can be as simple as a single word. Either way, it can jumpstart our writing, whether we are at the beginning or the middle of a project, whether we are free-writing in journals or writing fiction.

5-4-3-2-1 Write! is meant for speculative fiction writers. These prompts place us in urban fantasy settings or the far reaches of space. Some are complex scenarios, and some are just one word. The question "What if?" is always helpful when we use the shorter prompts. "Launch" may mean very little to us, but if we ask "What if the launch went wrong?" followed by "How could that happen?" then we may have something interesting to start us off. Of course, there may be many kinds of launches. What kind of "launch" is the prompt about? This is a question that only the writer can answer. A "launch" could be a space ship launch, a Viking war ship launch, a launch of a new fantastical quest, or the launch of a home-made catapult that sends its occupants into a new dimension. Prompts can act as tiny starting points in the mind of an imaginative writer.

Creativity is a something we can stretch by asking ourselves questions and working from a beginning point and out into an endless number of imaginative possibilities. These prompts are meant to start writers on a journey, to get us started, to help on those blank page days. The book is separated into five sections: Scenarios, Quotes, Titles, Questions, and Simple.

5-4-3-2-1-Write!

SCENARIOS

Scenarios give writer a scene, a few characters, and a dilemma. The following scenarios are each less than 120 words long, so a writer still has room to imagine and create possibilities.

Scenario#1

For as long as Rowan could remember, her dad had sung her to sleep. Even when she was old enough to have friends over, he sang them all to sleep. Plus, he insisted she have a night light in her room. The older she got, the more she realized this was strange, if not downright embarrassing. Then, one night, after pretending to go to sleep, she shut off her night light.

Within a few minutes, a shadowy figure appeared outside her window with a bag of sand in his hands. But, when he reached for her windowsill, she could see . . .

See what? How does our heroine, Rowan, fare against this shadowy villain?

Scenario #2

With a battered cookie sheet for a shield and a branch for a sword, Taylor fought the dark knight.

Laughter broke her concentration.

"Would you look at her! I told you she's crazy!"

Taylor took one look at her true enemies, and ran.

Rushing headlong through an overgrown set of bushes, she tripped over a root, and slammed into the back of a knight who looked like he had stepped out of the pages of Medieval Armor.

She back away and shook her head. Her imagination was never this good.

He held up his black-gauntleted fingers, and . . .

What happens next? What is Taylor's fate?

Scenario #3

Curling around his favorite toy, Dragos purred himself into a midday nap on the deck. His human, Gwendy, would be home soon to praise his silky mane, and he wanted to be thoroughly rested for the occasion.

Something flicked his nose.

Dragos woke to see a knight in flame-retardant armor standing before him.

"Wake, foul beast and take your true form so I might rescue the maiden you have ensorcelled!"

Dragos yawned and allowed his dragon form to flow outward. His inner fire rumbled in his chest.

The knight brandished his sword. "Avaunt!"

His charge was interrupted by Gwendy's arrival.

What happens next?

Scenario #4

Bay Shannon ran his fingers over the cracked console of the ancient fighter. As a child, he had fought imaginary battles with renegades. He had never imagined that he would become one.

His friend Jay's static-filled voice came from the radio at his hip, "B, you've got incoming."

"Got it."

Bay started the fighter's engines, and arced his fighter into the sky above his family's devastated fields.

Two corporate fighters streaked towards him.

Bay flew like a scared rabbit, hoping the C-fighters wouldn't bother to read his ship's infrareds.

Two streaks of plasma-fire rushed towards him.

What happens to Bay?

Scenario #5

Captain Sherlock of 221B Baker Streak and his first mate, Dr. Watson, were in trouble again. It had all started out as an innocent investigation of a not-so-innocent string of murders on Friza 3, third moon of Regus.

The murderer had the latest Class A Streak ship with weapons.

"Sherlock, I told you we needed missiles more than that science lab taking up space in cargo bay," Dr. Watson stated his obvious and redundant opinion, again.

Sherlock shrugged. "You'll just have to fly us out of here, Watson. Use your space navy skills."

Plasma fire struck the shields, weakening them.

What happens next?

QUOTES

In this section, writers will find quotes from various speculative fiction books. Try to write a new story from an old quote and see where it takes you. Readers will find the source of each quote on the Quote Source page at the back of the book, but I urge writers not to peek until they have written.

Quote #1

"Can you keep a secret?"

Quote #2

 "Time is a sea, breaking up on the shore of this moment; and with every ripple, with every wave, I remember."

Quote #3

"It was my aunt who decided to give me to the dragon."

#4 Quote

"He began his new life standing up, surrounded by cold darkness and stale, dusty air."

Quote #5

"Who can chart the vastness?"

QUESTIONS

Question prompts are often part-scenario prompts. Many writers find stories by asking questions.

Question #1

Who can see in the dark?

Question #2

Who walks on an empty road leading into the sea?

Question #3

Why walk in space without a tether?

Question #4

Who gives up a life to travel to distant galaxies, with no hope of return?

Question #5

What does dragon breath smell like?

BOOK TITLES

Book titles are a unique sort of prompt. If we are too familiar with their origin, we might want to re-tell the story. If that's the case, write it with a twist. If it's an unknown title, imagine the possibilities. Not all of the titles here are from speculative fiction books, but they can always find a new purpose with a new story.

Everyone Knows What a Dragon Looks Like

A Draw of Kings

Shadow Spinner

The Land I Lost

Double Negative

SIMPLE

Simple prompts are the toughest to use, requiring the most imagination and the most question-seeking of the writer because they are so simple. However, I like them best as a writer because they can go nearly anywhere. Take the word or words and write them on the blank page, and then write.

Lost islands

A star map

Flight deck

Launch

Portal

WRITE ON!

My favorite writing advice is perhaps the dullest and most-used one: just write.

It is truly the best way to become better at writing.

My second suggestion is: reading. Read what you like, and then write. The reading will seep into your own writing craft as you inherently start to understand plot, pacing, and characterization.

Third, I suggest reading craft books on writing. I have several favorites and I'm currently reading a few at the same time. For fantasy writers, I highly recommend writing books by Gail Carson Levine. I'm also a fan of *Save the Cat!,* which is a book on screenplay writing which can be applied to the general plot structure of fiction novels. There are many other writing books I like, but it would take me a while to name them all.

QUOTE SOURCES

#1 *The Tail of Emily Windsnap* by Liz Kessler

#2 *The Quest for Celestia* by Steven James

#3 *Dragon Slippers* by Jessica Day George

#4 *The Maze Runner* by James Dashner

#5 *Incarceron* by Catherine Fisher

ABOUT THE AUTHOR

Tyrean Martinson is a writer, daydreamer, believer, storyteller, and teacher. She has several books out at online stores, including at least one other writing prompt book. She can be found at her blog, on twitter, and many other online spaces.